W9-CAS-691

Churches ad hoc

A   D I V I N E   C O M E D Y

Herman Krieger

with a foreword by
Kern R. Trembath

McMasters United Methodist
Church Library

PhotoZone Press
Eugene, Oregon

Churches ad hoc

© 1998 Herman Krieger

All rights reserved. No part of the contents
of this book may be reproduced by any means
without the written permission of the publisher.

Published by
PhotoZone Press
PO Box 51024
Eugene, OR 97405

Printed in the United States of America

First Edition

Publisher's Cataloging in Publication Data

   Krieger, Herman
   Churches ad hoc : a divine comedy / Herman Krieger.

   p. cm.

   ISBN: 0-9665809-6-6

   1. Church buildings—Photography—Humor.
   2. Church in art.
   3. Photography—Church buildings—Social aspects.
   4. Wit and humor, Pictorial.

   TR659.K7 1998
   726.5   98-96488

Book and Cover Design by
Peter Holm, Sterling Hill Productions

F O R E W O R D

Most if not all readers will be amused by what lies inside this volume. Most will be, but for a wider variety of reasons than many books enjoy. And if you are among the latter, "amuse" will turn out to be too weak a word. "Beguile" will be more likely.

The first time you read this book, you will know that it is one of those that you will return to again and again in the future. Is it a book of photography? — of art more generally? — of puns? — of religious architecture? — of questionable, comic, and at times tragic religious architecture? The answer, of course, is "yes." Hence its beguiling nature and consequent beckoning to regular revisitation.

Herman Krieger describes himself as a non-practicing Jew who has not been to synagogue since he was 12. Would that all religious education "took" as well as his! The most obvious and, in many ways, most delightful interaction that he will quicken in you is that between caption and photo. And most of the captions will, in turn, be drawn either directly or indirectly from Jewish and Christian scriptures. Herman thus nicely illustrates the ancient insight, voiced by Ignatius Loyola but universally true, "give me a child until he is six and he will be a Catholic forever." Religious truths, often embodied in text but always pointing beyond the text to experience itself, rarely go away for good. At worst, they hibernate. In the gentle humor that *is* the conversation between caption and photo, this book might well awaken hibernating truths in you as well. Another beguiling level of meaning, therefore: not, "Will this re-awakening happen?" but rather, "Did Herman intend it?"

The puns in this book, that is, the multi-layered conversations between image and caption, are witty. I mean this in the widest possible sense, what the Oxford English Dictionary laboriously reminds us is "that quality of speech or writing which consists in the apt association of thought and expression, calculated to surprise and delight by its unexpectedness; the utterance of brilliant or sparkling things in an amusing way." Wit is thus the conjunction of the author's insight and foresight that opts to use humor as the conduit to the receiver's mind. How could anything other than wit better account for the effects of "The High and the Lofty," "Littergy," and the adjacent, "The Pope's Answer to Luther," and the "Sign of the Crossing?" These are not simply pictures with headings; indeed, they are sermons whose spiritual precision is the more appropriated (and enjoyed) the more that one patiently awaits it. Priests at Notre Dame have been known to be fired for exceeding 10-12 minutes per sermon. It was not until well after 10 minutes, though, that I finally got the point of the sermon entitled "Auto da Fe" (hint: look carefully at the car model and then at the bumper sticker). Jesus could not have been more concise.

What this volume ultimately is, then, is a book about what the catholic tradition terms "sacramentality," the insight that God's presence is mediated by any and all parts of creation, and hence that God is permanently as close, or as far away, as the individual wishes God to be. It is not that God is ever far away, though. All that the individual can accomplish is to recognize, or resist, that permanent adjacency. More than this is not given to us to do. Herman's volume shows us how perilously close that divine adjacency is on a daily basis. Easy to overlook, isn't it? Hence, all the more delightful to acquire.

A final illustration of this that I hope you will not resent. While embarking from vastly different shores, Herman and I share much of our respective journeys. We are both graduates of the University of California at Berkeley. We are both avid bicyclists, a habit nurtured at that same University. Computers are the primary "how" by which we serve our professions and our constituencies. We are both drawn to the subtle, the common, and the humorous as the means by which religion is seen as universally evident. I say this not to elevate myself to his level of insight, attentiveness, or artistry, but instead simply to add one closing picture to this volume. Thank you, Herman, for including me in it.

Kern R. Trembath, Assistant Chairman
The Department of Theology
The University of Notre Dame

INTRODUCTION

The genesis of *Churches ad hoc* was the photograph I made of a cross that seemed to rise up out of a tree. The cross, located in a park overlooking Eugene, Oregon, created a controversy regarding the separation of church and state. Proponents of the cross called it a war monument. Others saw it as a religious symbol. I titled the photograph "Propagation on the Mount." Thus began the series of captioned photographs with a cross as the unifying element. The series was first exhibited at the PhotoZone Gallery in Eugene.

Churches ad hoc was introduced on the Internet in 1996. Since then, references to it have appeared in a large number of Christian, as well as atheist, web sites. Each group seems to find a reflection of their own views in the captioned photographs. Excerpts from the series have appeared in places as diverse as the Internet edition of *The New York Times*, a Methodist church calendar, a rock band cassette cover, the religion page of the Stockholm *Svenska Dagbladet* newspaper, and a Cornell Law School poster for a national conference on *The Constitution and Religion: Theory and Practice*.

I take photographs to amuse myself as well as the occasional spectator. Exhibiting photographs for mutual pleasure is similar to a comedian telling jokes to an appreciative audience. But comedy is more serious than photography.

Herman Krieger, 1998

PROPAGATION ON THE MOUNT

CHURCH OF HIGH FIDELITY

ST. MARK VI MODEL

Littergy

THE POPE'S ANSWER TO LUTHER

SOCIETY OF FEATHERED FRIENDS

DOVES OF COLOR

FAR EASTERN ORTHODOX

THE HIGH AND THE LOFTY

FOR WHOM THE BELLS TOLL

IMMACULATE DELIVERY

PERISHIONERS MEETING PLACE

FETAL POSITION

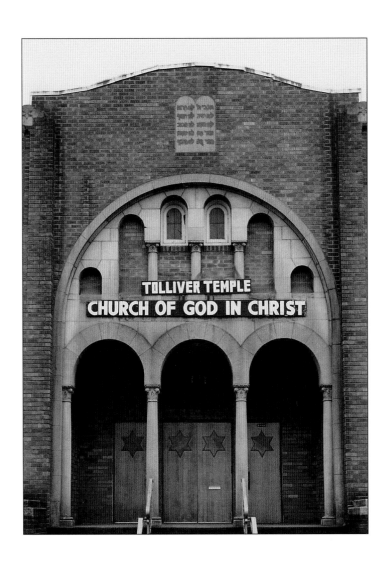

TEMPLE BETH TOLLIVER

WHEN THE SAINTS COME MARCHING IN

A POINT OF VIEW

ST. URBAN RENEWAL

VISITATIONS EXPECTED

FOLLOW THE STRAIGHT AND NARROW

Roadside Confessional

STATION OF THE CROSS

CHURCH OF THE RISING SON

ALL SEOUL'S CHURCH

DISESTABLISHMENT

DEFENDER OF THE FAITH

SHAKER SCHOOL

EASTER PROM

First United Methodist Church Library

27

TRY OUR FLUORIDATED BAPTISMS

MISSAL SILO

TEMPLE OF ANTENNA

WAITING FOR GODOT

HOLY ROLLER

Auto da Fe

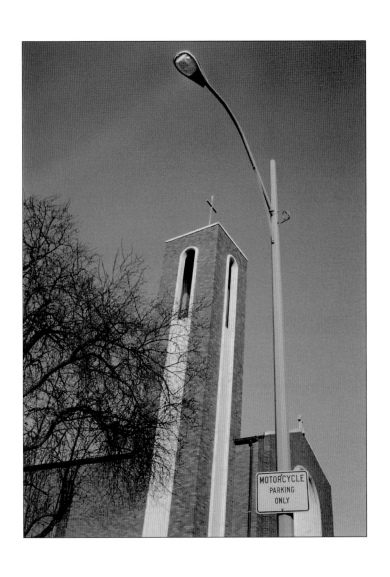

OUR LADY OF HELL'S ANGELS

NO OPIATE FOR THE MASSES

Carpal Deum

GLORY, GLORY, HALLELUJAH

CALIFORNIA GOTHIC

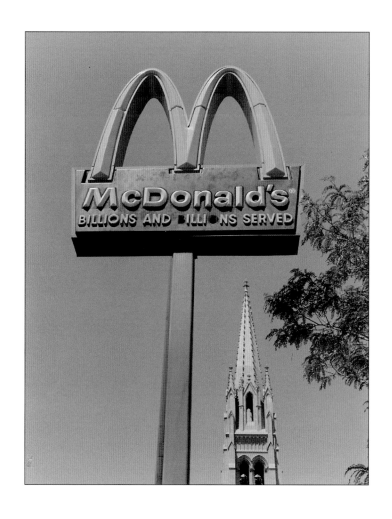

SIGNS OF THE TIMES

SINO QUA NON

TAO CROSS

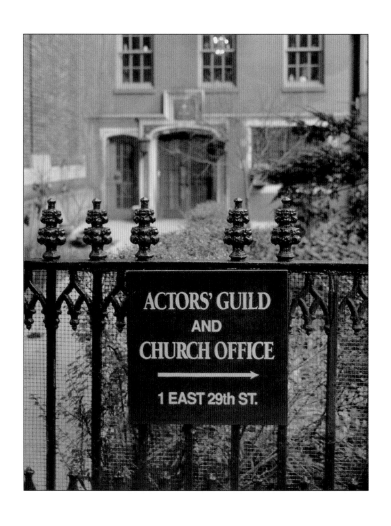

GETTING THEIR ACTS TOGETHER

PALM SUNDAY

FIRST CHURCH OF SALEM

CHRISTOPHER WREN HOUSE

UNISEXTARIAN

YOUNG ZIONIST

UNDER THE TREE OF HEAVEN

SELF-GUIDED TOURS
BEGIN IN GIFT SHOP

FOLLOW THE WISE MEN

49

TELECOMMUNION

THE LIGHT FROM ABOVE

SERMON ON THE MOUNT

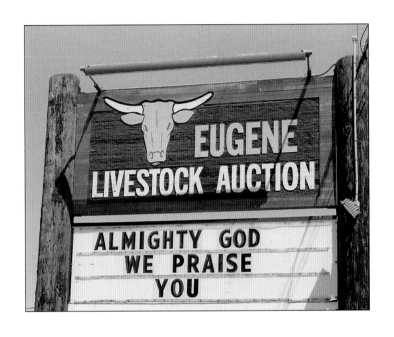

A<small>NGUS</small> D<small>EI</small>

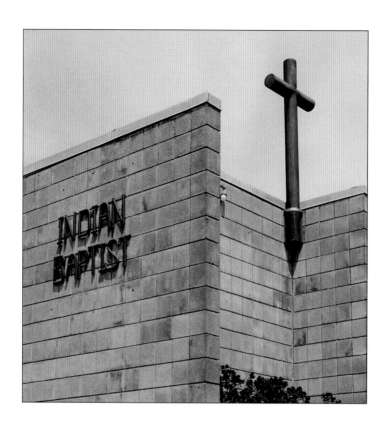

HALF-CREED

ENFORCED BY DIVINE POWER

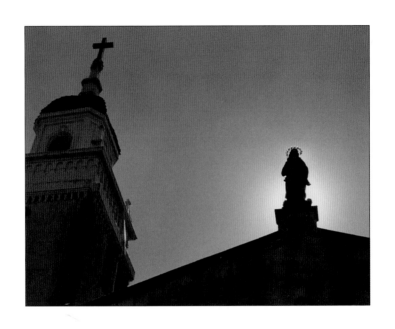

HALO MARY

ARCH ANGELS

LIBRARY OF CONGREGATION

Not for Mass Consumption

MASS TRANSPORTATION

WATCHTOWER

FAITH HEALING

Sound Doctrine

CRYPTOCOPTIC

ICONE

RO-DEO

MUST BE PC AND KNOW THY APPLES

RITUAL WASHING

ROAD TO REPENTANCE

JOHN THE BAPTIST

WAITING FOR A SIGN

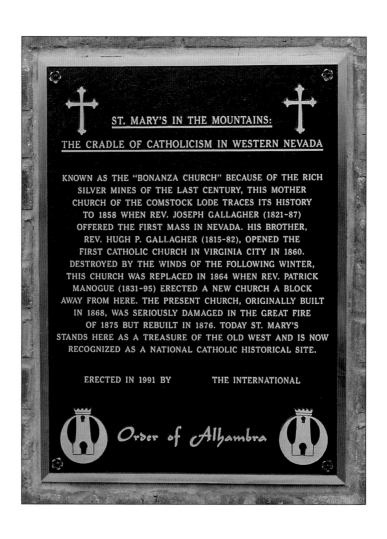

ST. MARY'S IN THE MOUNTAINS:
THE CRADLE OF CATHOLICISM IN WESTERN NEVADA

KNOWN AS THE "BONANZA CHURCH" BECAUSE OF THE RICH
SILVER MINES OF THE LAST CENTURY, THIS MOTHER
CHURCH OF THE COMSTOCK LODE TRACES ITS HISTORY
TO 1858 WHEN REV. JOSEPH GALLAGHER (1821-87)
OFFERED THE FIRST MASS IN NEVADA. HIS BROTHER,
REV. HUGH P. GALLAGHER (1815-82), OPENED THE
FIRST CATHOLIC CHURCH IN VIRGINIA CITY IN 1860.
DESTROYED BY THE WINDS OF THE FOLLOWING WINTER,
THIS CHURCH WAS REPLACED IN 1864 WHEN REV. PATRICK
MANOGUE (1831-95) ERECTED A NEW CHURCH A BLOCK
AWAY FROM HERE. THE PRESENT CHURCH, ORIGINALLY BUILT
IN 1868, WAS SERIOUSLY DAMAGED IN THE GREAT FIRE
OF 1875 BUT REBUILT IN 1876. TODAY ST. MARY'S
STANDS HERE AS A TREASURE OF THE OLD WEST AND IS NOW
RECOGNIZED AS A NATIONAL CATHOLIC HISTORICAL SITE.

ERECTED IN 1991 BY   THE INTERNATIONAL

Order of Alhambra

IT STARTED WITH 30 PIECES OF SILVER

SANCTUARY

T.G.I.F.

WINDOW DRESSING

IN VINO VERITAS

PORTAL TO PORTAL

MANY ARE CALLED, FEW ARE DIALED

TOWER OF BABBLE

KRISSCROSS

SIGN OF THE CROSSING

SERVICE ENTRANCE

SUN WORSHIPPERS

HELLFIRE FIGHTERS

THE VILLAGE GOLEM

REQUIEM